AF291168

Juan Gelman in Rome, 1979.
Photograph by Enrique Hernández-D'Jesús.

NOTES / NOTAS

BY

JUAN GELMAN

TRANSLATED FROM THE SPANISH BY

ARIANNA AFSARI AND SILVIA R. TANDECIARZ

Funded by
UK Government

Published 2026 by the87press
The 87 Press C.I.C.
87 Stonecot Hill
Sutton
Surrey
SM3 9HJ
www.the87press.co.uk

Copyright © Juan Gelman, 1979
English Translation Copyright © Arianna Afsari and Silvia R. Tandeciarz, 2026

The moral right of Juan Gelman has been asserted in accordance with the
Copyright, Designs and Patents Act 1988

ISBN: 9978-1-0684880-5-4

Printed and bound by CPI Group (UK) Ltd, Croydon, CR0 4YY

Cover image: *Manos anónimas* (1982-83), Carlos Alonso

Design: Stanislava Stoilova [www.sdesign.graphics]
Typeset in Otto (Instructions) and Arizona (Poems) by s-design. Otto is a custom font
designed by Sam de Groot and Lauren Opsomer Mironov and produced by Dinamo.
Arizona is a custom font designed by Elias Hanszer and produced by Dinamo.

EU GPSR Authorised Representative
LOGOS EUROPE, 9 rue Nicolas Poussin, 17000, LA ROCHELLE, France
E-mail: Contact@logoseurope.eu

Arianna Afsari is a translator and doctoral candidate in the Department of Comparative Literature at the University of Michigan (Ann Arbor). She examines Argentine militant poetry of the 1960s and 70s alongside traditions of Persian militant poetics deployed as tools of anticolonial resistance. Afsari works across three languages: Persian, Spanish, and Russian. As a translator, she has published English translations of selected poems and a preface from Juan Gelman's book, *Dibaxu*, in the literary translation journal, *Absinthe: World Literature in Translation* (December 2023).

Silvia R. Tandeciarz is Chancellor Professor of Modern Languages and Literatures and Vice Dean for Social Sciences and Interdisciplinary Studies at William & Mary, where she has worked since 1999. A translator, poet, and scholar in the field of Latin American Cultural Studies, she has published widely on the intersections between memorial and human rights initiatives in post-dictatorship Argentina. Her work in translation includes the critical treatises *Masculine/Feminine* (Duke University Press, 2004) and *The Insubordination of Signs* (Duke University Press, 2004), both by the Chilean theorist Nelly Richard, and the Poetry Book Society 2023 Translation Choice selection, *Sea in my Bones* (the87press), by Puerto Rican poet Juana Goergen.

To the memory of all those who struggled for liberation, for dignity, for justice. And to those taking up the struggle today, believing, as we do, that another world is possible.

Sin jactancias puedo decir
que la vida es lo mejor que conozco.

Without boasting I can say
that life is the best thing I know.
—FRANCISCO "PACO" URONDO

In the dark times, will there also be singing?
Yes, there will be singing.
About the dark times.
—BERTOLT BRECHT

CONTENTS

Introduction: The Resistance of Translation
and the Translation of Resistance by Arianna
Afsari and Silvia R. Tandeciarz 9

NOTES/NOTAS 31

NOTA I 34
NOTE I 35

NOTA II 36
NOTE II 37

NOTA III 38
NOTE III 39

NOTA IV 40
NOTE IV 41

NOTA V 42
NOTE V 43

NOTA VI 44
NOTE VI 45

NOTA VII 46
NOTE VII 47

NOTA VIII 48
NOTE VIII 49

NOTA VIX 50
NOTE VIX 51

NOTA X   52
NOTE X   53

NOTA XI   54
NOTE XI   55

NOTA XII   56
NOTE XII   57

NOTA XIII   58
NOTE XIII   59

NOTA XIV   60
NOTE XIV   61

NOTA XV   62
NOTE XV   63

NOTA XVI   64
NOTE XVI   65

NOTA XVII   66
NOTE XVII   67

NOTA XVIII   68
NOTE XVIII   69

NOTA XIX   66
NOTE XIX   67

NOTA XX   72
NOTE XX   73

NOTA XXI   74
NOTE XXI   75

NOTA XXII   76
NOTE XXII   77

NOTA XXIII   78
NOTE XXIII   79

NOTA XXIV   80
NOTE XXIV   81

NOTA XXV   82
NOTE XXV   83

NOTA XXVI   84
NOTE XXVI   85

NOTA XXVII   86
NOTE XXVII   87

THE RESISTANCE OF TRANSLATION AND THE TRANSLATION OF RESISTANCE

traducir es inhumano: ninguna lengua o rostro se deja traducir.
hay que dejar esa belleza intacta y poner otra para
acompañarla: su perdida unidad está adelante.

translation is inhuman: no tongue or face lets itself be translated.
you have to leave one beauty intact and supply another to go with it:
their lost unity lies ahead.

La traducción, ¿es traición?
La poesía, ¿es traducción?

Translation, ¿is it traitorous?
Poetry, ¿is it translation?

Juan Gelman[1]

Translation, especially of poetry, loves to resist.[2] Translators often experience the sensation that they are at war with both the original poem and their own translated version, which emerges wounded from the cross-linguistic battle, half what it once was. If we imagine translation as a dual struggle, one that unfolds in that contact zone between languages, what does it mean to translate a militant-poet who also rebels against his own language? What is the translator's responsibility to the resistance that powers the form and content of this poetry? And how might that tension best be captured to actualize its power?

Translating the poetry of Juan Gelman poses all these questions and

---

[1] The first epigraph is from "Exergo," *Com/posiciones* (Paris, 1984-85). Translation by Hardie St. Martin, *Dark Times Filled with Light* (Open Letter, 2012) 153-154. The second epigraph is from *Traducciones III. Los poemas de Sidney West* (1968-69) and attributed to Po I-Po, but this translation is our own. All unattributed translations in what follows are our own.

[2] Some sections of this co-written preface draw on revised material originally published by Arianna Afsari, "TOWARD A THIRD POETRY: Notes on Juan Gelman's Counterpoetry of Liberation and Anticolonial Resistance," in *Lit: Literature Interpretation Theory* 36, no. 2 (2025): 206–237, https://doi.org/10.1080/10436928.2025.2516399. The present rendition has been substantially reworked by the authors for the purposes of this book.

more. Born in 1930 to a family of revolutionaries—his father participated in the 1905 Russian Revolution before emigrating to Argentina—Gelman's political and poetic projects are inextricably entwined. Both figure prominently in the way he is remembered and studied today, not only in his native Argentina, but also around the world. In 1955, Gelman founded the militant poetry collective, El Pan Duro, along with several other committed Argentine poets including Juana Bignozzi and Héctor Negro. A year later, El Pan Duro published his first book of poems, *Violín y otras cuestiones* (*Violin and Other Questions*), marking the start of an enduring poetic trajectory consisting of over two dozen collections of poetry. It was also around this time that Gelman joined the Argentine Communist party and abandoned his university studies to work as an editor and a journalist.

By the early sixties, he was deeply engaged with leftist guerrilla organizations including the Fuerzas armadas revolucionarias (FAR, Revolutionary Armed Forces) and the Montoneros. In 1975 he was sent by the Montoneros to Rome to help denounce the escalating state-sponsored repression that anticipated Argentina's last dictatorship (1976-1983). Gelman would remain in exile for the rest of his life, witnessing from afar and yet feeling viscerally the pain and horror formally ushered in by the 24 March 1976 military coup d'état. In August of that same year, security forces came looking for him and instead detained and disappeared his son, Marcelo Ariel, and his pregnant daughter-in-law, María Claudia. Gelman would spend the next two and a half decades not only mourning his missing loved ones, but also searching for his granddaughter born in captivity. The eloquence with which he writes about his personal losses gives expression to the trauma experienced by tens of thousands who suffered similar horrors. By the dictatorship's end in 1983, the regime that persecuted, tortured, extrajudicially assassinated, and systematically disappeared any real or imagined political dissidents, would claim an estimated 30,000 lives, mostly civilians.

Wedding photo of María Claudia Iruretagoyena and Marcelo Gelman. Gelman Papers, Box B-000758.

While it would be a mistake to read Gelman's entire poetic trajectory through the prism of politics, equally problematic would be to ignore the contrapuntal movement between his activism and writing. As he expressed when accepting the 2007 Cervantes Prize—the most prestigious literary distinction in the Spanish-speaking world—his writing is part and parcel of a shared, generational struggle for a more just world: in the face of avoidable suffering, repression, and injustice, "ahí está la poesía: de pie contra la muerte" ("poetry is there: standing up to death").

Indeed, in his brief introduction to Gelman's poetry, "Contra las telarañas de la costumbre" ("Against the Spiderwebs of Custom," 1981), the renowned Argentine writer, Julio Cortázar, offers novice readers a useful guide for approaching this charged terrain. Recognizing the political undertow that characterizes Gelman's verse, Cortázar distinguishes it from the historical Marxist practice of "political poetry." Gelman's verses engage the territory of struggle not simply by describing and denouncing injustice, but rather by blowing up language—the Symbolic—altogether. In this way, his labor transforms poetry, itself, into a vehicle for liberation.

To appreciate the richness of Gelman's craft, readers must cast aside the spiderwebs of convention—preconceived notions regarding literary language, proper forms of address, accepted linguistic codes—and learn language anew. Only in so doing, through this process of deconstruction and construction, might the journey through his work yield a clear understanding of, and engagement with, the social and political conditions so in need of change. In Cortázar's formulation,

> Only by remaining open, allowing meaning to enter other doorways than those of syntactical structure or manufactured images, of metaphors or figures of speech that are more or less difficult but well established in poetic tradition—only in this way can the reader discover the reality of the poem, which is none other than the exact and literal reality of the horror and death, but also the hope, that define the Argentina of [the] times. Each will feel the same surprise at the ongoing transgressions encountered, one after the other, along the way, but only those who shoulder and somehow continue his methods will deserve a book that sets out to include [...] all of us.[3]

By destabilizing and estranging language, Gelman constructs a counterlanguage that exposes the systemic violence perpetrated against the Argentine masses: a polymorphic violence predicated on exclusion that precedes and extends beyond the military dictatorship, one that is also the atmospheric violence of late-stage capitalism and neocolonialism operating on a continental and global scale. This constitutes a significant historical detail that we, as contemporary readers and translators of *Notas*, must bear in mind: Argentina's repressive military Junta functioned within a broader clandestine campaign of neocolonization executed by several military regimes in the Southern Cone and backed by the United States. Under the code name, *Operación Cóndor* (Operation Condor), eight South American dictatorships joined to form a vicious network of transnational repression that covered four-fifths of the continent; their criminal operations targeting leftist political opponents

---

[3] Joan Lindgren, *Unthinkable Tenderness* (Berkeley: University of California Press, 1997), 4. Translation modified.

extended to Mexico, the United States, and Europe, and were aided in part with intelligence, financial assistance, and training in torture tactics provided by the CIA.[4]

The destruction in the poet's material realm finds expression in his writing through a series of violent experiments. As violence is registered in the text through mangled conjugations and compulsive slashes that rip sense apart, the gap between guerrilla fighter and poet, between militant logos and praxis, becomes blurred: "El poema cesa de ser comunicación para volverse contacto" ("The poem ceases to be communication in order to become contact").[5] By taking up the poetic front in the struggle against the unfreedom of a neocolonial reality, Gelman discovers his *own* counterlanguage, arising from a revolutionary worldview, one that is artfully summarized by the poet himself:

> La poesía cada vez más como actitud; la poesía en contradicción con un mundo—y que son palabras de uno de nosotros, Juan Gelman— que por su propia esencia niega toda poesía, contribuyendo a anticipar el otro mundo, el mundo de la poesía en libertad.

> Poetry increasingly as an attitude; poetry in contradiction with a world—and those are the words of one of our own, Juan Gelman— that out of its own essence rejects all poetry, contributing to the task of anticipating another world, the world of poetry in freedom.[6]

Cortázar's counsel to readers approaching Gelman's work in the Spanish original is even more important for those of us trying to capture or access his poetry in translation. We, too, must pay attention to the

---

[4] Operation Condor's South American member states included Argentina, Bolivia, Brazil, Chile, Ecuador, Paraguay, Peru, and Uruguay. For a well-documented account of this brutal campaign of repression in Latin America, see John Dinges' seminal study, *The Condor Years: How Pinochet and His Allies Brought Terrorism to Three Continents* (New York: New Press, 2004).

[5] Julio Cortázar, "Contra las telarañas de la costumbre," in *Interrupciones 1* (Buenos Aires: Seix Barral, 1997), 8.

[6] Carlos Alberto Brocato and José Luis Mangieri, *El pan duro. Grupo de poesía* (Buenos Aires, Ediciones La Rosa Blindada, 1963), 10.

stylistic techniques and radical experimentation with which the poet introduces "strangeness into the familiar space of language."[7] Beyond his unconventional approach to punctuation and capitalization, even more challenging for his translators are the ways in which Gelman upends the Spanish grammatical rulebook by pairing feminine articles with masculine nouns and vice-versa; by introducing intentional grammatical errors in verbal conjugations, imitating a type of childlike speech; and by manipulating nouns and patterns of verbal endings to invent words and create new meaning, such as *niñar* (to child), *enmorir* (to indeathen), and *vivimorir* (to livdie). The translation of *Notas* (*Notes*, 1979) before us is a case in point.

Published from exile following a three-year hiatus from poetry after the onset of the right-wing military coup in Argentina, *Notas* exemplifies one of the most admirable and paradoxical qualities of Gelman's poetry: "desde el exacto centro de la muerte, celebra la vida" ("from the exact center of death, he celebrates life").[8] Selections from this tamizdat anthology have been translated into English, but no translation of the full collection has been published to date. The text that follows represents our attempt to rectify this, heeding Cortázar's observation that "to embark upon these poems is to embark upon a path, following its curves and slope, stopping where the path appears to end in crossroads and resuming the journey as each poem takes up from the preceding one."[9] Too much is lost when the poem is lifted out of context, because "one and only one poem is born from the sum of the poems. The last one reveals the first as the first one the last, and each is a step in the progression of the path. To let oneself be borne along is to come closer with each page to that overview that suddenly crystallizes both the previous stages and the final purpose."[10] To grasp the full import of Gelman's work, to hear his voice, one must be open

---

[7] Kate Jenckes, "Juan Gelman's Open Letters: Mourning and Mundo Beyond Militancy," *CR: The New Centennial Review* 14, no. 1 (Spring 2014): 162, https://doi.org/10.14321/crnewcentrevi.14.1.0153.

[8] Eduardo Galeano, "Apuntes para una cara, armada con pedazos de este libro," in *Interrupciones 1* (Buenos Aires: Seix Barral, 1997), 14.

[9] Cortázar, "Contra las telarañas de la costumbre," 3.

[10] Ibid., 3–4.

to the journey; this translation brings this possibility to English-speaking audiences for the first time.

A quick reading of "Nota I" can help clarify what respecting the sequence of the original and approaching the collection as a whole make possible. "Nota I" operates as a type of preface that anticipates the themes, names, and style that readers will encounter in the verses that follow. From the very first line of this initial poem, Gelman announces one of his main intentions behind the collection: "te nombraré veces y veces" ("I'll name you again and again"). The *vos* (you) of his address is identified only once and midway through this first poem as *derrota* (defeat), a defeat most profoundly materialized in the bodies of the fallen. In this sense, these opening lines function as a type of dedication to Gelman's *compañeros* killed and disappeared by the terrorist State.[11] Although the poet names his beloved dead "again and again" throughout the twenty-seven poems that comprise *Notas*, it is only here in this first poem that everyone is named together. Not only does "Nota I" list the names of each of his dearly departed, including his missing son, grandchild, and fellow committed writers Rodolfo Walsh, Francisco "Paco" Urondo, and Haroldo Conti; it also invokes them to imagine and plot a series of intense actions against their collective defeat, repeating his promise "te mataré" ("I'll kill you") or "te voy a matar" ("I'm going to kill you") a total of eleven times. The lyric voice here prefers the verb *matar* (to kill) over the adjective *muerto* (dead), which appears more frequently in the poems that follow. Through this emphasis on the verbal, *on the call to action rather than mere description*, we discover an unwavering resolve to deliver on the speaker's drive to vanquish defeat through creative expression and active recollection.

Let us feel the proximity of tenderness and violence in "Nota I" below:

---

[11] The reader will no doubt notice that the word *compañero* has been left in the original Spanish in our English translations. The Spanish word *compañero* possesses a whole range of possible meanings, including, but not limited to, "friend," "comrade," "companion," and "classmate." Often in Gelman's poetry, *compañero* defies any one specific designation, instead encompassing many possible categories. Therefore, our decision to leave *compañero* untranslated is a deliberate one, for the English options available to us impose unnecessary restrictions to the broader, more capacious Spanish term, ultimately limiting the reader's freedom in interpreting the poetry in English.

te nombraré veces y veces.
me acostaré con vos noche y día.
noches y días con vos.
me ensuciaré cogiendo con tu sombra.
te mostraré mi rabioso corazón.
te pisaré loco de furia.
te mataré los pedacitos.
te mataré uno con paco.
otro lo mato con rodolfo.
con haroldo te mato un pedacito más.
te mataré con mi hijo en la mano.
y con el hijo de mi hijo/muertito.
voy a venir con diana y te mataré.
voy a venir con jote y te mataré.
te voy a matar/derrota.
nunca me faltará un rostro amado para matarte otra vez.
vivo o muerto/un rostro amado.
hasta que mueras/
dolida como estás/ya lo sé.
te voy a matar/yo
te voy a matar

I'll name you again and again.
I'll lay with you night and day.
nights and days with you.
I'll defile myself fucking your shadow.
I'll show you my rabid heart.
I'll trample you crazed with fury.
I'll kill your little pieces.
I'll kill one of you with paco.
another I kill with rodolfo.
with haroldo I kill you one piece more.
I'll kill you with my son in hand.
and with the son of my son/little dead one.
I'm coming with diana and I'll kill you.
I'm coming with jote and I'll kill you.
I'm going to kill you/defeat.
never will I lack a beloved face to kill you again.
alive or dead/a beloved face.

until you die/
hurt as you are/I already know.
I'm going to kill you/I
am going to kill you

Our translation interprets the *vos* that Gelman repeatedly assails in these opening verses as the internalized sense of defeat, brokenness, and alienation experienced by those left behind, that animates a psychological violence turned inwards, against the self. This antagonistic *vos* can also be understood as the Junta's killing machine that in late twentieth-century Argentina functioned through covert executions and clandestine disappearances. Vowing to continue the fight that swallowed up a whole generation of militant *compañeros* means venturing into that enemy territory of State terrorism, dredging up from the shadows its criminal operations, and materializing its illogical terror into a visceral foe. Within an alienating world of abstractions, "where for too long art is cut off from the concrete facts—which, from the neocolonialist standpoint, are accusatory testimonies," Gelman foregrounds the death and destruction that saturate his homeland's every day.[12]

Indeed, the word "dead," or some variation of it, whether verb, noun, or adjective, appears in twenty of the twenty-seven *Notas*. Even where "death," "dead," or "to die" are not explicitly referenced, Gelman appeals to morbid imagery to evoke violence and slaughter. He never, however, utilizes the words *ausente* (absent), *ausencia* (absence), or even *desaparecido* (disappeared). The notable lack of these terms reveals the poet's refusal to adopt the State's "lexicon of terror."[13] Thus, he combats the oppressor's official discourse that sought to permanently erase its victims with the phrase *ausentes para siempre* (the forever absent). By speaking of the living, Gelman talks of hope. By speaking of the dead, he talks of a concrete crime that has been committed at the hands of the dictatorship and demands justice. In

---

[12] Octavio Getino and Fernando Solanas, "Toward a Third Cinema," *Cinéaste* 4, no. 3 (1970): 123, http://www.jstor.org/stable/41685716.

[13] We reference here Marguerite Feitlowitz's groundbreaking study, *A Lexicon of Terror: Argentina and the Legacies of Torture* (Oxford: Oxford University Press, 1998).

this way, he resists the liminal condition of the disappeared, fruit of the oppressors' violence, instead capturing absence strictly in terms of life and death.[14] The lyric voice of the grieving militant—at times purposeful, at times probing—compels his readers to locate themselves in "el espejo de nuestra verdadera realidad argentina" ("the mirror of our true Argentine reality"), to take a position, and to consider how the power of poetry, and of remembrance, might deliver a form of revolutionary justice beyond the State.[15]

Nowhere is this clearer than in Gelman's invocation of those he's lost. If initially he swears to kill defeat, as a lone actor—a task that can only be accomplished through the repeated slaughter of its constitutive *pedacitos* (little pieces), as captured here, "te mataré los pedacitos" ("I'll kill your little pieces")—his vows in the middle section carry the absent others, whom he individually names. Each fragment of the *vos* must be killed *with* the help of the dead or alive *compañeros*. Alone, the mission is impossible. The poetic voice demonstrates an awareness of his reliance on the other until the difficult task at hand is completed:

> nunca me faltará un rostro amado para matarte otra vez.
> vivo o muerto/un rostro amado.
> hasta que mueras/
>
> never will I lack a beloved face to kill you again.
> alive or dead/a beloved face.
> until you die/

In this way, Gelman transforms his beloved phantoms into dominant actors, substituting a poetry of passivity with one of open rage. His verses resuscitate his comrades, Paco, Rodolfo, Haroldo, Diana, Jote, and Gelman's son, all combatants crushed by the regime, with the reader

---

[14] In 1979, military Junta leader, General Jorge Rafael Videla, responded to a question about the victims of State terrorism by describing the category of the missing as follows: "No tiene entidad, no está ni muerto ni vivo, está desaparecido" ("They have no identity, they are neither dead nor alive, they're disappeared"). A year later, Roberto Viola, the military commander who succeeded Videla as de facto President, dubbed the country's detained and disappeared persons *ausentes para siempre* (the forever absent).

[15] Cortázar, "Contra las telarañas de la costumbre," 10.

serving as a witness to their rebirth. Their refiguring, taking violence back into their own hands, invokes the logic of Frantz Fanon: "The very same people who had it constantly drummed into them that the only language they understood was that of force, now decide to express themselves with force."[16] The spectral living-on of the dead found throughout *Notas* shifts and takes the shape of real human beings whose sacrifices are not lost in the past. In fact, they have *not even passed*. Their lives and struggle continually fuel those of the still living, including but not limited to, the necessary counterviolence directed against the neocolonizing forces of the present. In Gelman's own words when introducing some of the poems that comprise *Notas*, "Fui compañero de oficio y de combate de Rodolfo [Walsh]. Por ese privilegio leo lo que él escribió en mí, sus marcas, lo que ayuda a vivir: estos poemas" ("Rodolfo and I were brothers in arms and in profession. For that privilege I read what he wrote in me, his traces, what helps with living: these poems).[17] Indivisible in a struggle that continues, only together might they help secure a less alienated future.

Photo of Juan Gelman (center, standing) with Francisco "Paco" Urondo (left of Gelman) and musician, Juan "Tata" Cedrón (center, seated), in Mendoza, Argentina, 1965. Gelman Papers, Box B-000759.

---

[16] Frantz Fanon, *The Wretched of the Earth*, trans. Richard Philcox (New York: Grove Press, 2004), 42.

[17] Gelman speech, accepting an award at the Facultad de Periodismo y Comunicación Social, Folder 3, "Apuntes," 1998. Gelman Papers, Box B-000717.

Both a recognition of defeat and a call to arms, Gelman's opening poem thus illuminates the arc of the whole, inviting his readers into the imagined community of collective memory by generating a kind of shared intimacy that is conducive to caring, and hence, to action. John Berger's formulation of the labor of poetry captures beautifully what is at stake for Gelman and for us, as the translators of *Notas*: "Poetry can repair no loss, but it defies the space which separates. And it does this by its continual labour of reassembling what has been scattered [...] To break the silence of events, to speak of experience however bitter or lacerating, to put into words, is to discover the hope that these words may be heard, and that when heard, the events will be judged."[18] Addressed to death and mourning, the collection presents a perfect case study for understanding Gelman's craft, the masterful way in which he bends language to express a Symbolic order deformed by violence and also to generate the conditions for something new. Death itself becomes a construction in Gelman's lyric, a fertile terrain for new beginnings. This paradoxical notion illustrates how out of an atmospheric neocolonial violence comes the interconnectedness of past and present struggles against a capitalist totality, illuminating the capacity for solidarity to defy temporal and spatial boundaries.

In translating him, we have chosen to follow the poet's lead rather than operate from the safe confines of our own linguistic conventions. For example, in the fourth *Nota*, Gelman formulates his own verb, *enmorir*, riffing off similar verbs in Spanish like *envejecer* (to grow old), *ensuciar* (to make dirty), and *enloquecer* (to drive insane), to describe the experience of being completely submerged or in (*en*) the act of dying (*morir*). As a survivor in this broken world plagued by absent *compañeros*, the poet ponders:

> ¿qué estoy haciendo con los miles yo
> de compañeros muertos?
>
> ¿me estoy enmuerteando yo?

---

[18] John Berger, "The Hour of Poetry," in *And Our Faces, My Heart, Brief as Photos* (London: Writers and Readers, 1984), 96-98.

> ¿what am I doing with the thousands
> of dead compañeros?
>
> ¿am I indeathening me?

Breaking up the fabricated gerund—*enmuerteando*—the inquisitive statement hardens into a moment of recognition of his pained reality: *en/muerte/ando yo* (in/death/I go, or in/death/I am). We can also think of *enmuerteando* as capturing the disjointed temporality of mourning, a spectral moment, that defies our normal sense of time. *Enmuerteando* allows for the possibility of being, both spatially and temporally, in one's own mortality and in that of the other. In our translation, we opted to mimic the poet's wordplay by creating our own verb, "indeathen," and conjugating it into the gerund as "indeathening." With these choices, we strive to capture the sensation of being enveloped in death, of having one's being gradually and fundamentally altered by death, as is suggested by *enmorir*. We found, in other words, that by mirroring Gelman's de/constructive process and not literally translating *enmuerteando* as "indeathgoing" or "indeathbeing" we were able to better approximate the rhetorical possibilities of the original.

Gelman's unorthodox orthography and *grafía* (graphic expression) pose additional moments for creative and radical experimentation that we have chosen to meet in the same way. The journey through *Notas* not only moves readers between feelings of grief and rage, but also doubt, fear, and even joy and tenderness. Ambiguity is everywhere in the form of numerous unanswerable questions. There are even poems that are entirely made up of questions, such as "Nota IV." Our choice to keep the inverted question marks from the original Spanish is driven in part by our wish to facilitate the reader's engagement, making it more obvious where Gelman's questions puncture and disrupt the text. By retaining the upside-down question marks, our translations bear traces of the language in which *Notas* was first composed. We insist on the affect that they convey as well as honor the poet's own wishes regarding the unconventional *grafía* so characteristic of his writing, as captured in a handwritten request by Gelman to his editors found among his papers at Princeton University:

Gelman's full note reads: "A quien corresponda. Se ruega respetar la grafía, a veces inusual, de estos textos. Muchas gracias." ("To whom it may concern. Please respect the graphic expression, at times unusual, of these texts. Thank you very much"). Gelman Papers, Box B-000713.

At its core, "Nota IV" amplifies a fundamental question that also propels what comes after it: learning how to live with the ghosts—those absent others—whose spectral presence continually informs the present. The nature of mourning in Gelman's poetry is not simply about an experience of individual loss, but also about how we relate to alterity. This is precisely why in "Nota IV" he characterizes mourning as a "sufrir propio y ajeno" ("suffering ours and others'"). Like in "Nota I," the poet employs the idea of "pieces" to trace a continuity between past and present, between the self and the other. In addition to lamenting the death of his loved ones, he mourns himself in this *vos* (you), indicating how these "other pieces" compose the essence of his own life. Indeed, if we break down the word "remembering," we discover that the process involves reuniting the scattered fragments of the self in order to reconstitute the whole: *re-member-ing*. The dictatorship's official discourse, based on erasure, denied the very possibility of remembrance, and consequently, of repair. By putting the pieces of a ruptured self back together again, Gelman engages in a more visceral and embodied form of remembrance beyond the limits of the State:

¿juntos como anduviéramos ahora
sin sufrir propio y ajeno?

¿pero por qué me lloro en vos-
otros pedazos de mi vida?
¿acaso puedo al fin llorar?
¿puedo por fin al fin llorar?

¿together how would we be now
without suffering ours and others'?

¿but why do I cry myself in you-
all pieces of my life?
¿is it that I can finally cry?
¿at last can I finally cry?

Gelman's questioning does more than introduce doubt; it conjures those vanquished *compañeros* to fracture the totalizing silence and disavowal of the dictatorship, specifically its disappearance of its own citizens. The combatant-poet shocks the lethargy of his readers, spurring us to call everything into question. As Cortázar reflects, "Cuando Juan pregunta se diría que nos está incitando a volvernos más lúcidamente hacia el pasado para después ser más lúcidos frente al futuro" ("When Juan asks questions, one could say that he is inciting us to turn more lucidly toward the past so that later we can be more lucid when facing the future").[19] Gelman's interrogation of the events of the past, particularly the sacrifices made by his *compañeros*, calls forth their continual presence and futurity.

One more example from "Nota IV" may be useful for illustrating the importance of respecting Gelman's *grafía* to capture both meaning and affect. In the final stanza, Gelman deploys punctuation and wordplay in one of his typical language games to signal the continuity between the spheres of living and dead. The dash attached to the word *vos* stands out in part because this is the only time a dash appears in lieu of a slash

———————————

[19] Cortázar, "Contra las telarañas de la costumbre," 10.

in all twenty-seven poems. The verse following *vos-* begins with the word *otros* (others). Gelman's subtle trick here rests on the possibility, indicated by the uniqueness of the dash, of joining the words *vos* and *otros* to create the second-person plural, *vosotros*. In other words, it is possible to read these verses in the following two ways: the first consists of a singular, second-person interlocutor, or *vos* (you), whereas the second suggests a plural presence, or *vosotros* (you all).[20] The two possible readings are illustrated below:

> ¿pero por qué me lloro en vos-
> otros pedazos de mi vida?

> ¿pero por qué me lloro en vosotros
> pedazos de mi vida?

To keep this wonderful game and the ambiguity it implies in the English version, we opted for a mistranslation of "vos- // otros" as "you- // all" over the literal translation, "you- // others." Translating loosely rather than exactly here permits the English language reader the freedom to creatively experiment with Gelman's language, since it is possible to read the "you" as singular or plural, as demonstrated in English below:

> ¿but why do I cry myself in you-
> all pieces of my life?

> ¿but why do I cry myself in you all
> pieces of my life?

If punctuation is generally intended to help readers make sense of what they are reading, in Gelman's masterful deployment, it also graphically expresses a world shaped by violence. As in the above example, where Gelman uses a dash to indicate the splitting open of a *vosotros* into

---

[20] It should be noted that although *vosotros* is frequently preferred in Spain as a manner of informal, plural address and not in Argentina (or Latin America, for that matter), Gelman's use of the *vosotros* form here establishes a sense of intimacy and familiarity between the lyrical voice and his interlocutors that the more formal *ustedes* (you all), more common in Latin American Spanish, does not convey.

disaggregated and alienated parts of a whole, his much more liberal use of the punctuative slash blows open the dichotomy between life and death to link these two traditionally opposed concepts. In multiple poems, he presents a phrase containing the word *vida* (life), then introduces a slash in the middle of the verse, following the break with another phrase that mirrors the first one but instead presents its opposite, *muerte* (death), thereby forming a parallel construction with two contradictory terms.

In "Nota XIV," for example, Gelman questions the whereabouts of his disappeared son with slashes and neologisms, casting us into that zone where negations are annulled and binaries rupture:

> ¿estás vivo?/¿estás muerto?/¿hijo?/
> ¿vivimorís otra vez/otro día/como
> moriviviste estos tres años
> en un campo de concentración?/¿qué
>
> hicieron de vos/hijo/dulce calor que alguna vez
> niñaba al mundo/padre de mi ternura/hijo
> que no acabó de vivir?/¿acabó de morir?/
> pregunto si acabó de morir/el nacido el morido
>
> ¿are you alive?/¿are you dead?/¿son?/
> ¿do you livdie again/another day/like
> you dielived these three years
> in a concentration camp?/¿what
>
> did they make of you/son/sweet warmth that once
> childed the world/father of my tenderness/son
> who never finished living?/¿did he finish dying?/
> I ask if he finished dying/the born the deadparted

In this sense, the punctuative slash marks that liminal space between life and death, the only place where one can aspire to learn to live, following Jacques Derrida's suggestion: "Neither in life nor in death *alone*. What happens between two, and between all the 'two's' one likes, such as between life and death, can only *maintain itself* with some ghost, can only *talk with or about* some ghost."[21] In other instances, Gelman casts aside the slash altogether to completely collapse the separate, traditionally juxtaposed, words into his own invented terminology, grouped together on one side of the slash, as exemplified by invented verbs like *vivimorís* (you livdie) and *moriviviste* (you dielived) as well as intentional grammatical errors such as "el nacido el morido" ("the born the deadparted").

As the above examples illustrate, the poet's aesthetic innovations in Spanish coupled with our commitment to remain true to his approach have compeled us to battle against the neat confines of our own language—English. To stage our rebellion against English, to deconstruct it and ultimately construct *our own* counterlanguage, we have had to give ourselves over to the twists and turns of Gelman's craft. Following Gayatri Spivak's invitation to "surrender to the linguistic rhetoricity of the original text," we have made a conscious decision to prioritize his stylistic experiments over producing easily legible translations.[22] Mending his disjointed style, re-ordering his convoluted syntax, and erasing his compulsive punctuations risk neutralizing, even deadening, the most compelling aspects of his work: the call to engagement that keeps bringing us back to him, again and again. Instead, by paying attention to the specific rhetoricity of Gelman's unorthodox language play, we honor the revolutionary labor of his de/construction, its political urgency, its rupturing and generative power.

In this way, we also recognize the relations of force that exist between us and *Notas*. After all, we translate Gelman from within the *palacios del Imperio* (palaces of Empire), constitutive of "la academia gringa," and into the language most closely associated with the neocolonial violence his poetry denounces.[23] As Spivak warns, "Without a sense of

---

[21] Jacques Derrida, *Specters of Marx: The State of the Debt, the Work of Mourning, and the New International*, trans. Peggy Kamuf (New York: Routledge, 1994), xvii.

[22] Gayatri Chakravorty Spivak, "The Politics of Translation," in *The Translation Studies Reader*, 4th ed. (London: Routledge, 2021), 323.

[23] Silvia Rivera Cusicanqui, *Ch'ixinakax utxiwa: una reflexión sobre prácticas y discursos descolonizadores* (Buenos Aires: Retazos, 2014), 57.

the rhetoricity of language, a species of neo-colonialist construction of the non-western scene is afoot."[24] Our hope is that these translations, which attend to Gelman's stylistic revolutions and combatant rhetoricity, represent a decolonizing practice that brings English-language audiences into contact with the emancipatory gesture of the original; and that they fuel global anticolonial solidarity by opening spaces for encounters with other "pockets of resistance" that can lead to transformation and, perhaps, even a form of justice.[25]

---

[24] Spivak, "The Politics of Translation," 322.

[25] John Berger, "Against the Great Defeat of the World," in *The Shape of a Pocket* (New York: Vintage International, 2003), 213.

A quien corresponda

Se ruega respetar la grafía, a veces inusual, de estos textos.
Muchas gracias.

Juan Gelman

NOTAS
[CALELLA DE LA COSTA/PARÍS/ROMA, 1979]

NOTES
[CALELLA DE LA COSTA/PARIS/ROME, 1979]

A Eduardo Galeano
A Helena

To Eduardo Galeano
To Helena

NOTA I

te nombraré veces y veces.
me acostaré con vos noche y día.
noches y días con vos.
me ensuciaré cogiendo con tu sombra.
te mostraré mi rabioso corazón.
te pisaré loco de furia.
te mataré los pedacitos.
te mataré uno con paco.
otro lo mato con rodolfo.
con haroldo te mato un pedacito más.
te mataré con mi hijo en la mano.
y con el hijo de mi hijo/muertito.
voy a venir con diana y te mataré.
voy a venir con jote y te mataré.
te voy a matar/derrota.
nunca me faltará un rostro amado para matarte otra vez.
vivo o muerto/un rostro amado.
hasta que mueras/
dolida como estás/ya lo sé.
te voy a matar/yo
te voy a matar

NOTE I

I'll name you again and again.
I'll lay with you night and day.
nights and days with you.
I'll defile myself fucking your shadow.
I'll show you my rabid heart.
I'll trample you crazed with fury.
I'll kill your little pieces.
I'll kill one of you with paco.
another I kill with rodolfo.
with haroldo I kill you one piece more.
I'll kill you with my son in hand.
and with the son of my son/little dead one.
I'm coming with diana and I'll kill you.
I'm coming with jote and I'll kill you.
I'm going to kill you/defeat.
never will I lack a beloved face to kill you again.
alive or dead/a beloved face.
until you die/
hurt as you are/I already know.
I'm going to kill you/I
am going to kill you

NOTA II

ya que moría mañana
me moriré anteanoche/
con un cuchillo fino
voy a cavar el 76
para limpiarle las raíces a paco
las hojitas a paco
clavado al suelo como una mula rota

gente me quería ayudar/
después le toca al 77
para encontrar los ojos de rodolfo
como cielos terrestres
fríos fríos fríos
diseminados por ahí/
mirada vacía ahora

va a haber que trabajar
limpiar huesitos/que no hagan
negocio con la sombra
desapareciendo/dejándose ir
a la tierra ponida sobre
los huesitos del corazón/
compañeros denme valor/

la sombra vuela alrededor
como un objeto en mi pieza/
ni remedio que la pueda parar/
ni corazón ni nada/
ni la palabra nada/
ni la palabra corazón/
pañeros/compañeros.

NOTE II

since I was dying tomorrow
I'll die the night before last/
with a fine knife
I'll dig up '76
to wipe the roots off paco
the little leaves off paco
nailed to the ground like a broken mule

people wanted to help me/
next it's '77's turn
to find rodolfo's eyes
like terrestrial skies
cold cold cold
scattered about/
a now empty gaze

there's work to be done
cleaning little bones/so they don't
trade with the shadow
disappearing/giving in
to the earth putted over
the little bones of the heart/
compañeros give me courage/

the shadow flies around
like an object in my room/
no remedy to stop it/
no heart no nothing/
not even the word nothing/
nor the word heart/
panions/companions.

NOTA III

andar con las rodillas desnudas
por un campo de vidrios rotos/
andar con el alma desnuda
por un campo de compañeros rotos/

que no los mojará el atardecer
ni el mar que moja a cualquiera/
no sé qué los moja ahora/
por fin quietos/sin miedo

a la muerte/muertos/
por plomo o por cianuro/por
mano propia o ajena/muertos
en todo caso/podridos

bajo tierra en la tierra
que sí los recibió/incendios
que apagó el odio militar/hijitos
empújennos al triunfo

NOTE III

to wander with bare knees
through a field of broken glass/
to wander with soul bared
through a field of broken compañeros/

who won't be soaked by sunset
nor by the sea which soaks anyone/
I don't know what soaks them now/
still at last/without fear

of death/dead/
by lead or by cyanide/by
their own hand or another's/dead
in any case/rotten

underground in the ground
that did receive them/fires
the military hatred put out/little children
push us toward victory

NOTA IV

el temor a la vejez ¿envejece?
el temor a la muerte ¿enmuerta?
¿qué estoy haciendo con los miles yo
de compañeros muertos?

¿me estoy enmuerteando yo?
¿acaso les temo/amados?
¿te acaso temo paco/cara
como una alegría humana?

¿o los envidio yo tal vez?/
¿o los envidio yo tal vez?/
¿juntos como anduviéramos ahora
sin sufrir propio y ajeno?

¿pero por qué me lloro en vos-
otros pedazos de mi vida?
¿acaso puedo al fin llorar?
¿puedo por fin al fin llorar?

NOTE IV

the fear of old age ¿ages?
the fear of death ¿indeathens?
¿what am I doing with the thousands
of dead compañeros?

¿am I indeathening me?
¿is it that I fear you/loved ones?
¿is it that I fear you paco/face
like a human happiness?

¿or do I envy you all perhaps?/
¿or do I envy you all perhaps?/
¿together how would we be now
without suffering ours and others'?

¿but why do I cry myself in you-
all pieces of my life?
¿is it that I can finally cry?
¿at last can I finally cry?

NOTA V

no echés a la tristeza del fogón/
siéntese aquí a mi lado/vieja/
usté nunca me va a dejar/
perdoneme si la olvidé

si anduve de rabia en rabia
saliendo de un muerto entrando
a otro muerto o mundo roto/
si así viajé por estos años/

arrímese/tristeza/que
me hace frío tanta furia
y tanto puerto muerto y
necesito viajar/viajar

don't chase sorrow from the campfire/
sit here by my side/old lady/
you'll never leave me/
forgive me if I forgot you

if I moved from rage to rage
leaving one dead entering
another dead or broken world/
if I travelled like this through these years/

come closer/sorrow/for
I'm chilled by so much fury
and so many dead harbors and
I need to travel/to travel

NOTA VI

me pregunto qué sería
de la belleza de rodolfo ahora/
esa belleza en vuelo lento
que le iba encendiendo ojos/

si volaría o no volaría
esta vez que nos derrotaron
por soberbios y ciegosordos
pero tal vez sí volaría/

o volaría triste triste
corriendo el mundo con la mano
para mostrar los compañeros
que cayeron por la belleza

NOTE VI

I wonder what would be
of rodolfo's beauty now/
that beauty in unhurried flight
that bit by bit lit up his eyes/

if it would fly or not fly
this time we were defeated
by the proud and blinddeaf
but perhaps it would fly/

or fly sorrowful sorrowful
shifting the world by hand
to reveal the compañeros
who fell for beauty

NOTA VII

ya no te quiero/furia/
no te quiero más/rabia
me desolás el corazón/
me volvés ciego el corazón

y yo necesito que
la claridad me bese como
amor donde amo mi acabar
como empezar/vení tristeza/

matame vos los muertos que
mochileo con toda el alma/
o terminalos de matar

ya que la gente sigue/como
paisaje o voz que no se calla/
gente que no termina más

NOTE VII

I no longer want you/fury/
I don't want you anymore/rage
you devastate my heart/
you turn my heart blind

and I need
clarity to kiss me like
love where I love my ending
like beginning/come sorrow/

kill the dead for me that
I carry with all my soul/
or finish killing them

since people go on/like
a landscape or voice that doesn't quiet/
people with no end

NOTA VIII

hasta mañana/compañeros/ahora
ustedes siguen las lógicas del muerto/
la pudrición/la descomposición/
hasta mañana hasta mañana/

aplaudiría al pajarito
que se volara de vos/rodolfo/
después de haber comido sangre
que resbalaba por tus lentes/

a la iguana llena de luz
que revisó las entrañas del
haroldo y comió de haroldo/
iguana rápida de luz/

será mañana que veamos
o nos veamos/no nos veamos/
o sea que muerto yo alcanzara
a ver tu talón/paco/brillar

bajo el suelo donde yacés
con calavera pensativa
por nosotros/pobres de vos/
talón nocturno crepitando

como políticas rabiosas
para matar al enemigo
hoy absolutamente hoy/
talón que pisa el tiempo y parte/

o vivo nos veamos mañana
ni siquiera en el triunfo o
los umbralitos del triunfar/
bastaría encontrarse en

el compañero cara de uno
que nos juntara como yunta/
como ternura/como valor/
hasta mañana hasta mañana

NOTE VIII

until tomorrow/compañeros/now
you follow the logic of the dead/
the rotting/decomposing/
until tomorrow until tomorrow/

I'd applaud the little bird
that flew from you/rodolfo/
having eaten the blood
that slid over your glasses/

and the iguana full of light
that inspected the entrails of
haroldo and ate of haroldo/
iguana quick of light/

it'll be tomorrow that we see
or see each other/not see each other/
or rather dead that I manage
to see your heel/paco/shine

under the ground where you lie
with skull contemplative
of us/impoverished of you/
nocturnal heel rattling

like politics raging
to kill the enemy
today absolutely today/
heel that hurries time and splits/

or alive we see each other tomorrow
not even in triumph or
the tiny thresholds of triumphing/
it would suffice to meet in

the compañero face like ours
that would yoke us together/
like tenderness/like valor/
until tomorrow until tomorrow

NOTA IX

talmente llovió sangre/
sangre llovió por mi país
de las venas que el verdugo cortó/
del corazón que las recuerda/

hermanos en la sangre a navegar
cada día cada día cada día/
este viajar no nos conduce
al paraíso ni al infierno/

no vamos al paraíso/
no vamos al infierno/
¿adónde vamos/sangre/
que cantás amada en la noche?

¿o como pájaro volás
de sangre a sangre/recordando/
o sea gorrión de resistir
al olvido/que ni una gota seque?

así navegamos/ciegos/
para que nadie se secase/
o volara de sangre a sangre
y pudiera cantar/cantar

NOTE IX

likethis blood rained/
blood rained through my country
from the veins cut by the torturer/
from the heart that remembers them/

brothers in blood off to sail
each day each day each day/
this voyaging does not take us
to paradise nor to hell/

we're not going to paradise/
we're not going to hell/
¿where are we going/blood/
that you sing beloved in the night?

¿or like a bird you fly
from blood to blood/remembering/
or like a sparrow of resistance
to oblivion/so that not a single drop dries up?

like this we sailed/blind/
so that no one would dry up/
or fly from blood to blood
and could sing/sing

NOTA X

¿dónde queda el país donde todos se reúnen?
¿atrás/alante/abajo/arriba/queda ese país?
por ahora en la muerte todos se reúnen
por ahora se reúnen en la muerte/atrás

del que dejaron/del que barajaron/abajo
de los que amaron/sombras
reunidas de una vez/país
donde los todos se reúnen/salvo

al tiempo que vendrá/más justo/
donde juntarse vivos y muertos/
que quisieron la libertad/
que te quisieron/libertad/

NOTE X

¿where is the country where everyone gathers?
¿is that country behind/before/below/beyond?
for now in death everyone gathers
for now they gather in death/behind

the one they left/the one they shuffled/below
those they loved/shadows
gathered at last/country
where the everyones gather/save

a time yet to come/more just/
where living and dead join together/
all those who wanted freedom/
who loved you/freedom/

NOTA XI

¿a la memoria le falta realidad/a la
realidad le falta memoria?/¿qué hacer
con la memoria/con la realidad

en la mitad de esta derrota o alma?/
alma a quien todo un pueblo sangre ha sido/
del olvido nace una flor gorda marrón/

resignaciones nacen/sujeciones/
pudriciones/de la memoria crecen resistencias/
agravios/daños/padeceres/todo

lo que el alma no puede perdonar/nacen bellezas/pajarito
que sufriste volando por esta tierra o sur/
grave como olvidar la realidad

es que la realidad olvide/porque nosotros
amados/pajaritos/ustedes
que la sufrimos/que la somos

en carne propia/en propia luz o fuego/
donde fuegamos con dolor/
con hijitos/con sueños/con clavículas/

podridos bajo la bota militar/
¿qué tenemos?/¿un sapo en la boca?/del cementerio/
la memoria/¿no sacamos muertitos

como pedazos de vos/nos/
ayeres/ayes/desesperos?/alguno
¿quiere tacharnos realidad?/¿la

realidad tacha/habida cuenta
de ignorancias mezquindades/cegueras
de la Revolución/abajada/

tocada/manoseada/ensuciada
por la Razón de Estado de la Revolución?/
¿y cuál es el estado

de la razón de la revolución?/¿en qué está?/¿tacha
la realidad de la memoria/la memoria de la realidad?/
igual seguís/crepitás/Revolución/amora mía/amora nuestra/luz

NOTE XI

¿does memory lack reality/does
reality lack memory?/¿what is to be done
with memory/with reality

in the midst of this defeat or soul?/
soul for whom a whole people have been blood/
from forgetting a fat brown flower is born/

resignations are born/adherences/
rottings/from memory resistances grow/
grievances/damages/sufferings/all

that the soul cannot forgive/beauties are born/small bird
that you suffered flying across this earth or south/
as grave as forgetting reality

is for reality itself to forget/because we
beloved/little birds/you
who endure it/we who are it

in our own flesh/in our own light or fire/
where we infire with pain/
with little children/with dreams/with clavicles/

rotten under the military boot/
¿what do we have?/¿a toad in our mouths?/from the cemetery/
memory/¿didn't we take the little dead

like pieces of you/ours/
yesterdays/ohs/despairs?/anyone
¿want to redact reality for us?/¿does

reality redact/having accounted for
the ignorance pettiness/blindness
of the Revolution/debased/

groped/felt up/sullied
by the Revolution's Reason of State?/
¿and what is the state

of the revolution's reason?/¿what is it up to?/¿does it cross out
the reality of memory/the memory of reality?/
still you carry on/crackling/Revolution/inloving of mine/inloving our/light

NOTA XII

A Manuel Scorza

los sueños rotos por la realidad
los compañeros rotos por la realidad/
los sueños de los compañeros rotos
¿están verdaderamente rotos/perdidos/nada/

se pudren bajo tierra?/¿su rota luz
diseminada a pedacitos bajo tierra?/¿alguna vez
los pedacitos se van a juntar?
¿va a haber la fiesta de los pedacitos que se reúnen?

y los pedacitos de los compañeros/¿alguna vez se juntarán?
¿caminan bajo tierra para juntarse un día como dice manuel?/
    ¿se juntarán/un día?
de esos amados pedacitos está hecha nuestra concreta soledad/
per/dimos la suavidad de paco/la tristeza de haroldo/la lucidez
    de rodolfo/el coraje de tantos

ahora son pedacitos desparramados bajo todo el país
hojitas caídas del fervor/la esperanza/la fe/
pedacitos que fueron alegría/combate/confianza
en sueños/sueños/sueños/sueños/

y los pedacitos rotos del sueño/¿se juntarán alguna vez?
¿se juntarán algún día/pedacitos?
¿están diciendo que los enganchemos al tejido del sueño general?
¿están diciendo que soñemos mejor?

NOTA XII

To Manuel Scorza

dreams broken by reality
compañeros broken by reality/
the compañeros' dreams broken
¿are they truly broken/lost/nothing/

do they rot underground?/¿their broken light
disseminated to bits underground?/¿someday
will the bits and pieces join together?
¿will there be a party for the little pieces that reunite?

and the pieces of the compañeros/¿will they someday join together?
¿do they walk underground to join together one day as manuel says?/
    ¿will they join together/one day?
of those beloved pieces our concrete solitude is made/
we mis/gave the gentleness of paco/the sadness of haroldo/the lucidity
    of rodolfo/the bravery of so many

now they are little pieces scattered under the whole country
small fallen leaves of fervor/hope/faith/
bits and pieces that once were joy/combat/trust
in dreams/dreams/dreams/dreams/

and the broken pieces of the dream/¿will they join together someday?
¿will you join together one day/bits and pieces?
¿are you asking that we hook you into the fabric of the general dream?
¿are you asking that we dream better?

NOTA XIII

cada compañero tenía un pedazo de sol/
en el alma/el corazón/la memoria/
cada compañero tenía un pedazo de sol/
y de eso estoy hablando

no estoy hablando de los errores que
nos llevaron a la derrota/por ahora/no
estoy hablando de la soberbia/la ceguera/el delirio militarista
    de la conducción/
estoy diciendo que cada compañero tenía un pedazo de sol

que le iluminaba la cara/
le daba calor en el pavor nocturno/
lo abellaba alegrándole los ojos/
lo hacía volar/volar/volar/

¿se apagaron esos pedazos de sol ahora?/ahora que los compañeros
    murieron/¿se
apagaron sus pedazos de sol?/¿no siguen alumbrándoles
alma/memoria/corazón/calentándoles
el calcañar los huesos disparados de sombra?

solcito que se apagaba así/
todavía alumbrás esta noche/
en que estamos mirando la noche
hacia el lado por donde sale el sol

NOTE XIII

each compañero had a piece of sun/
in their soul/their heart/their memory/
each compañero had a piece of sun/
and of that I am speaking

I am not speaking of the errors that
led us to defeat/for now/I am not
speaking of the arrogance/the blindness/the militaristic delirium
    of the leadership/
I am saying that each compañero had a piece of sun

that illuminated their face/
kept them warm in their nightly dread/
inbeautied them with happiness in their eyes/
made them fly/fly/fly/

¿have those pieces of sun now dimmed?/now that the compañeros
    died/¿did
the pieces of sun dim?/¿don't they still light up their
soul/memory/heart/warming their
heels the bones shot through with shadow?

small sun that dimmed like this/
you still light up this night/
in which we gaze upon the night
in the direction of the sunrise

NOTA XIV

A Julio Cortázar

¿estás vivo?/¿estás muerto?/¿hijo?/
¿vivimorís otra vez/otro día/como
moriviviste estos tres años
en un campo de concentración?/¿qué

hicieron de vos/hijo/dulce calor que alguna vez
niñaba al mundo/padre de mi ternura/hijo
que no acabó de vivir?/¿acabó de morir?/
pregunto si acabó de morir/el nacido el morido

a cada rato/niño
que andó temprano por la sombra/voz
que mutilaron/ojo
que vio/niñito de mi sed arrancado

a sus pedazos/a su sed/las sedes
que le abrigaban corazón/
se lo encendían mesmamente/
toda la noche golpéandome la puerta

NOTE XIV

To Julio Cortázar

¿are you alive?/¿are you dead?/¿son?/
¿do you livdie again/another day/like
you dielived these three years
in a concentration camp?/¿what

did they make of you/son/sweet warmth that once
childed the world/father of my tenderness/son
who never finished living?/¿did he finish dying?/
I ask if he finished dying/the born the deadparted

at every turn/child
who wandered early in shadow/voice
they mutilated/eye
that saw/small child of my thirst torn

to his pieces/to his thirst/the thirsts
that harbored his heart/
set it alight veridly/
all night knocking at my door

NOTA XV

yo quisiera saber qué misterio había entre nosotros/
compañeros/combatientes/maravillas al sol/
sol ellos mismos/ofertados
a la vida/a la muerte/al misterio del tiempo que vendrá/

¿eh compañeros?/empezamos temprano a criticar
los e/horrores de la conducción nacional/el sectarismo/
    el triunfalismo/el
militarismo fatal/sin embargo seguíamos
ofertados a la vida/la muerte/¿qué misterio humilde

nos atacaba el corazón/tejido
con dolores/corajes/dudas/corazón/
abierto al tiempo que vino/a nuestro pueblo que
sufre y ya no debiera sufrir más?/compañeros

que ese misterio hizo vivir/morir/
y vos/cuerpo que aguanto/¿hasta cuándo me vas a aguantar?/
¿vas a aguantar la sangre que me cae en el alma?/sangre
de compañeros misteriosos me moja/

compañeros/incandescencias que
queman el aire alrededor
de estas palabras que piso
para tratar de respirar

NOTE XV

I'd like to know what mystery lay between us/
compañeros/combatants/marvels in the sun/
sun they themselves/offered up
to life/to death/to the mystery of a time to come/

¿hey compañeros?/early we began criticizing
the e/horrors of the national leadership/the sectarianism/
    the triumphalism/the
fatal militarism/and yet we carried on
offered up to life/to death/¿what humble mystery

attacked our heart/woven
with aches/braveries/doubts/heart/
open to the time that came/to our people who
suffer and shouldn't suffer any longer?/compañeros

who made that mystery live/die/
and you/body I endure/¿how long will you endure me?/
¿will you endure the blood that drips in my soul?/blood
of mysterious compañeros soaks me/

compañeros/incandescences that
burn the air around
these words I tread
trying to breathe

NOTA XVI

la furia que persigue al alma/
la tristeza que persigue a la furia/
la muerte que persigue a la tristeza/
¿o son muertes concretas?/¿paco

que se murió concretamente?/¿tristeza
por la muerte de paco?/¿furia
de paco muerto?/¿alma
que no resigna su memoria?/¿memoria

que la muerte cargó/la tristeza/la furia?/
¿paco que sueña/o pedacito
que me soñás/alma furiosa/país
que va reuniendo su dolor?

NOTE XVI

the fury that chases the soul/
the sorrow that chases the fury/
the death that chases the sorrow/
¿or are they concrete deaths?/¿paco

who died concretely?/¿sorrow
for the death of paco?/¿fury
of a dead paco?/¿soul
that does not resign his memory?/¿memory

that the death carried/the sorrow/the fury?/
¿paco who dreams/or little piece
that dreams me/furious soul/country
that is gathering its pain?

NOTA XVII

entre otras cosas/la derrota
es fuente de toda humildad/confirma
la humildad de los compañeros que
cayeron por el pueblo/amándolo/

compañeros sucios de sangre
que comprendieron y sufrieron/
en la memoria acostaditos
para seguir buscando luz

NOTE XVII

among other things/defeat
is the source of all humility/it confirms
the humility of the compañeros who
fell for the people/loving them/

bloodstained compañeros
who understood and suffered/
tucked away in memory
to go on searching for light

NOTA XVIII

A Fernando Birri

estamos vivos/entre compañeros
caídos por delación o combate/envueltos
en la intensidad de morir por el mundo/solos
o cada vez más solos bajo la noche clandestina/es decir

respira el pecho tristeza/
arden los huesos con tristeza/
yo me llamo tristeza/
son tristes la paloma y la tórtola

que tortolea en la paloma/
con pies de triste pisa la tristeza
la noche donde los compañeros vivos aún
rostros fosforescentes vemos como astros

subir/volar/callar a pedacitos/
lámparas de la ciega libertad
que reventó ojos amados
para que salga toda luz

NOTE XVIII

To Fernando Birri

we're alive/among compañeros
cut down by betrayal or combat/wrapped up
in the intensity of dying for the world/alone
or increasingly alone under the clandestine night/that is to say

the breast breathes sorrow/
the bones burn with sorrow/
my name is sorrow/
sorrowful are the pigeon and the dove

that doves in the pigeon/
with sorrowful feet sorrow treads
the night where the compañeros alive still
phosphorescent faces we see like stars

rise/fly/hush to bits and pieces/
lamps of the blind freedom
that burst beloved eyes
for all light to pour out

NOTA XIX

A Jorge Cedrón

hombre/la vida es algo
miserable/inmortal/abridora
de heridas y dolores/pero hombrísimo/
mirala deshacer
padecimientos como buey humano
que arase al otro lado de la sombra/
o te me amase la trasluz
para sufrir parejamente

NOTE XIX

To Jorge Cedrón

man/life is something
miserable/immortal/opener
of wounds and pain/but oh man/
watch her undo
afflictions like a human ox
plowing on the other side of the shadow/
or kneading for me your gleam
to suffer evenly

NOTA XX

no bajo a los infiernos/subo
hasta mi hijo clausurado
en su bondad/belleza/vuelo/
y torturado/concentrado/

asesinado/dispersado
por los dolores del país/
¿algún fueguito crece de
la gran silencio de tus ojos?/

oigo la noche caminar
por tus huesitos/duelen/huelen
a tu menor pisado/a
la palomita que tenías

tornasolándote la voz
de hijito solo por la guerra/
por la mitad/por las provincias
desiertas del puro dolor/

hijo que nadie hará otra vez/
golpeo las puertas de la muerte
para desalojarte de
hechos que no te corresponden

NOTE XX

I don't descend to the infernos/I go up
to my son foreclosed
in his kindness/beauty/flight/
and tortured/concentrated/

assassinated/dispersed
within the country's pain/
¿any firelight grow from
the great silence of your eyes?/

I hear the night walking
through your little bones/they hurt/smell
of your lightest footsteps/of
the little dove you kept

iridescenting your child's
voice left alone by war/
split in half/in the provinces
deserted from pure pain/

son no one will ever make again/
I beat on the doors of death
to dislodge you from
events you don't deserve

NOTA XXI

A Gerardo

a ver carita mía/levantada
de los polvos de la derrota/me
duelen los muertos que me traés/o luna/
lucecita que brilla en la medula

de tu levantamiento general
contra la muerte/cara/¿qué querés?/
¿estás borracha de dolor o viento
que los huesitos de los compañeros

vientan en esta noche mineral/
como pared donde están escribidos
los nombres de roqué/jote/la diana/

los demás compañeros como bueyes
arando sombras de su destrucción
para que comprendamos de una vez?

NOTE XXI

To Gerardo

let's see my dear face/lifted
from the dust of defeat/the
dead you bring hurt me/or moon/
shimmering light in the marrow

of your general uprising
against death/face/¿what do you want?/
¿are you drunk on pain or wind
that the compañeros' little bones

are winding in this mineral night/
like a wall writparted with the
names of roqué/jote/la diana/

the other compañeros like oxen
plowing shadows of their destruction
so that we might understand once and for all?

NOTA XXII

huesos que fuego a tanto amor han dado
exilados del sur sin casa o número
ahora desueñan tanto sueño roto
una fatiga les distrae el alma

por el dolor pasean como niños
bajo la lluvia ajena/una mujer
habla en voz baja con sus pedacitos
como acunándoles no ser/o nunca

se fueron del país o patria o puma
que recorría la cabeza como
dicha infeliz/país de la memoria

donde nací/morí/tuve sustancia/
huesitos que junté para encender/
tierra que me entierraba para siempre

NOTE XXII

bones that fire to so much love have given
exiles from the south without home or number
now they undream so many broken dreams
a weariness distracts their soul

they wander through pain like children
under the foreign rain/a woman
speaks in a low voice to her little pieces
as if cradling them not to be/or never

did they leave the country or homeland or puma
that roamed the head like
an unhappy happiness/country of memory

where I was born/died/had substance/
little bones that I gathered to ignite/
earth that inearthened me forever

NOTA XXIII

muertos que hablo y que me hablan
en las palabras que palabro/
estas mismas palabras que
cierran mi voz como una noche/

o como rostros compañeros
que giran bellos de su luz
como palabras/como sombras
apalabrándose a la muerte

NOTE XXIII

dead that I speak and that speak to me
in the words that I word/
these same words that
close my voice like nightfall/

or like companion faces
spinning beautiful from their light
like words/like shadows
giving their word to death

NOTA XXIV

a la derrota o ley severa mi
alma sabió perder respeto/te amo/
cruza mi alma la agua fría donde
flotan los rostros de los compañeros

como envolvidos de tu piel la suave
o lámpara subida delicada
para que duerman delicadamente
subidamente en vos/llama que nombra

a cada sombra por su nido/dicha
o soledad de fuego para amor
donde descansen bellos los mis muertos

que siempre amaron rostros como vos
donde tu rostro avanza como vos
contra la pena de haber sido/ser

NOTE XXIV

for defeat or severe law my
soul knowed to lose respect/I love you/
cold water crosses my soul where
the faces of compañeros float

as if inobliviated in your skin the soft
or lamp lifted delicate
so they might sleep delicately
liftedly in you/flame that names

each shadow by its nest/joy
or solitude of fire for love
where they might rest the beautiful my dead

who always loved faces like you
where your face carries on like you
against the pain of having been/of being

NOTA XXV

queridos compañeros/moridos
en combate o matados a traición o tortura/
no los olvido aunque ame a una mujer/
no los olvido porque amo/como

ustedes mismos amaron una vez/¿se recuerdan?/
¿bellos andaban por el aire?/¿y combatían?/
¿y el calor de una mujer les asomaba
en la cara?/¿se recuerdan?/me acuerdo

de haberles visto una mujer brillar
en medio del combate doloroso/
inmortales brillaban ustedes
contra el dolor/contra la muerte/

ahora que duermen calladitos
y alguna sombra dulce los tocara
acomodándolos mejor
contra los perros del olvido

NOTE XXV

dear compañeros/deadparted
in combat or killed by betrayal or torture/
I don't forget you though I love a woman/
I don't forget you because I love/like

you yourselves once loved/¿remember?/
¿beautiful you wandered through the air?/¿and battled?/
¿and the heat of a woman peered
from your face?/¿remember?/I recall

having seen in you a woman shine
in midst of painful combat/
immortal you shined
against pain/against death/

now that you sleep silently
and some sweet shadow might touch you
arranging you better
against the hounds of oblivion

NOTA XXVI

A Alberto Cedrón

los viandantes/¿no son bienandantes?/los
bienaventurados/¿no son biaventurados o
gallos que pisan porvenir
en la violenta madrugada?/corazón

que molés dioses en el aire
para panes de amor/¿sabés latines?/
¿o será pena que camisa madres
para el invierno que vendrá?

NOTE XXVI

To Alberto Cedrón

the waywalkers/¿aren't they goodwalkers?/the
goodfortuned/¿aren't they bifortuned or
roosters stepping on futures
in the violent dawn?/heart

that grinds gods in the air
for loaves of love/¿do you know latins?/
or is it pain that shirts mothers
for the winter that will come?

NOTA XXVII

A Vanni Blengino

de lo posible a lo probable/del
sueño a la realidad hay como
mares/playas nocturnas donde
animales de pico descarnan

formas mojadas por los jugos
del corazón/así/viajamos
del pecho al seco sol que dora
la maravilla/o existir

NOTE XXVII

To Vanni Blengino

from the possible to the probable/from
dream to reality there seem to be
seas/nocturnal shores where
beaked beasts dismember

forms drenched by the juices
of the heart/like this/we venture
from the chest to the dry sun that gilds
the marvel/or existing

?